DISNEY DUETS

ISBN 978-0-7935-6950-2

HAL•LEONARD®
CORPORATION
7777 W BLUEMOUND RD PO BOX 13819 MILWAUKEE, WI 53213

Visit Hal Leonard on the internet at http //www halleonard com

CANDLE ON THE WATER

from Walt Disney's PETE'S DRAGON

SECONDO

Words and Music by AL KASHA
and JOEL HIRSCHHORN

Smoothly, with expression

CANDLE ON THE WATER
from Walt Disney's PETE'S DRAGON

PRIMO

Words and Music by AL KASHA
and JOEL HIRSCHHORN

Smoothly, with expression

SECONDO

PRIMO

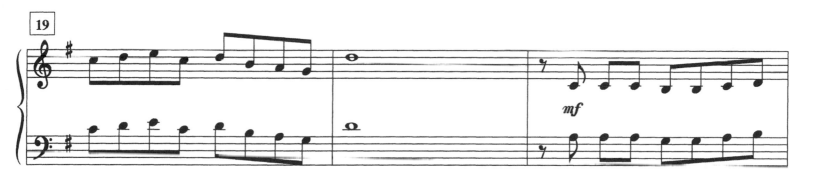

SECONDO

PRIMO

SECONDO

PRIMO

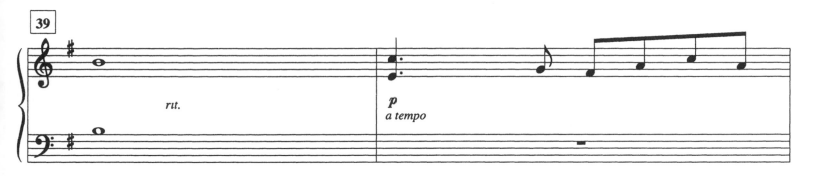

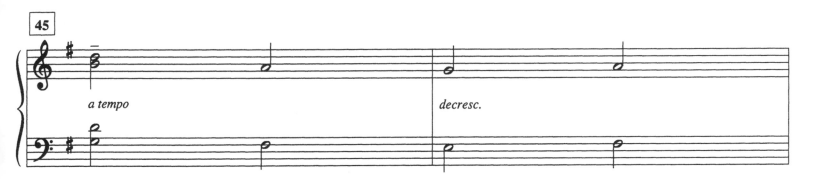

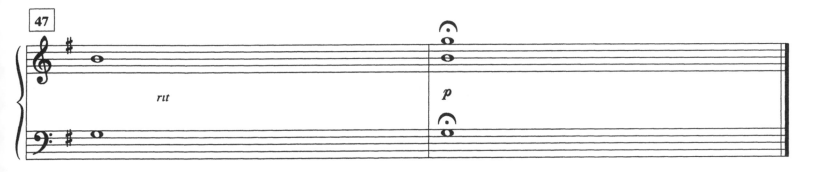

COLORS OF THE WIND
from Walt Disney's POCAHONTAS

SECONDO

Music by ALAN MENKEN
Lyrics by STEPHEN SCHWARTZ

COLORS OF THE WIND
from Walt Disney's POCAHONTAS

PRIMO

Music by ALAN MENKEN
Lyrics by STEPHEN SCHWARTZ

Moderately, with expression

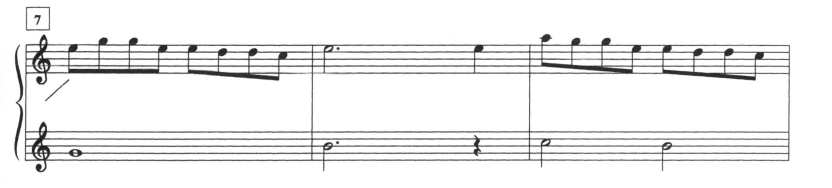

12

SECONDO

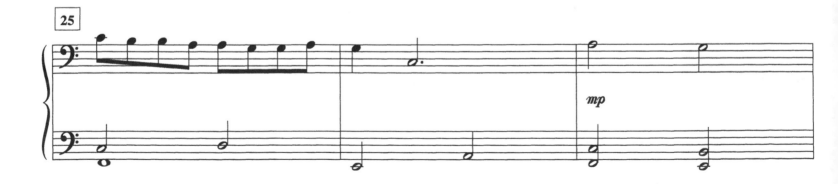

PRIMO

SECONDO

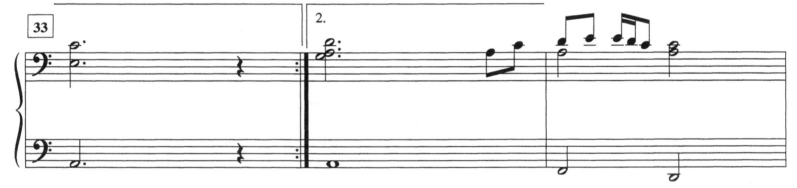

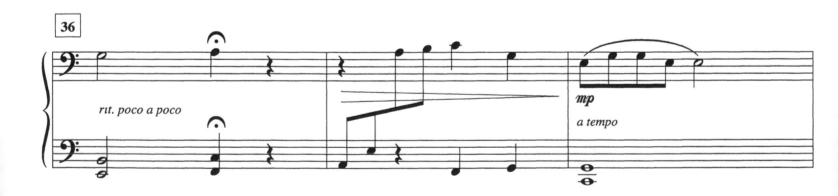

PRIMO

CRUELLA DE VIL
from Walt Disney's 101 DALMATIANS

SECONDO

Words and Music by
MEL LEVEN

Moderate swing rhythm

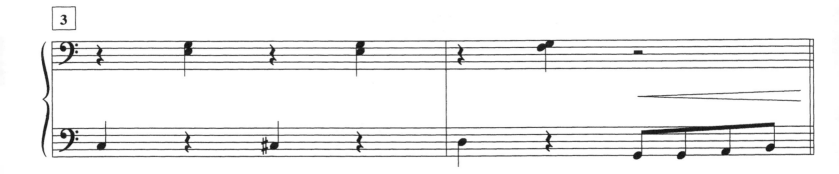

CRUELLA DE VIL
from Walt Disney's 101 DALMATIANS

PRIMO

Words and Music by
MEL LEVEN

Moderate swing rhythm

SECONDO

PRIMO

PRIMO

SECONDO

HAKUNA MATATA
from Walt Disney Pictures' THE LION KING

SECONDO

Music by ELTON JOHN
Lyrics by TIM RICE

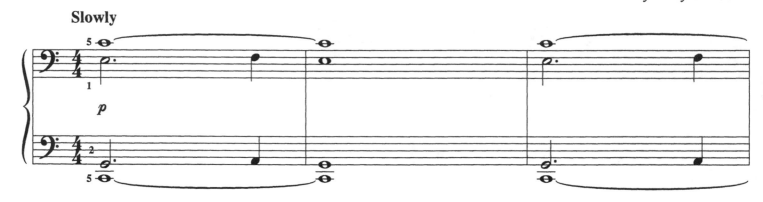

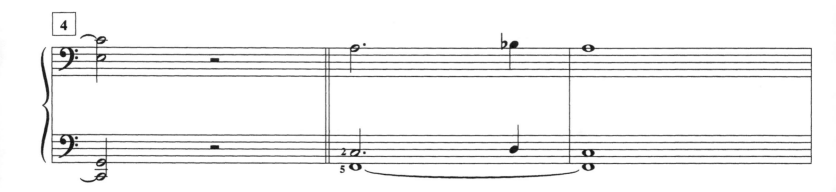

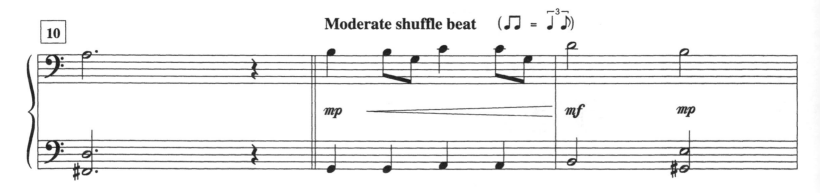

HAKUNA MATATA
from Walt Disney Pictures' THE LION KING

PRIMO

Music by ELTON JOHN
Lyrics by TIM RICE

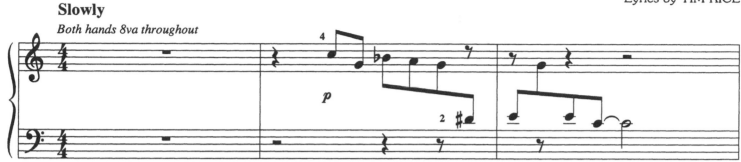

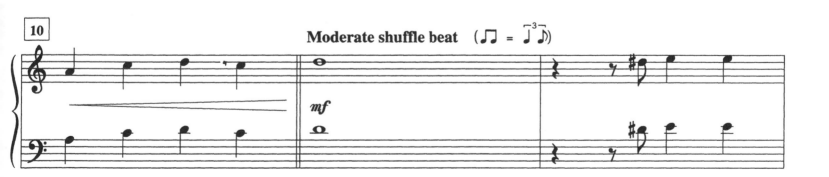

SECONDO

PRIMO

SECONDO

PRIMO

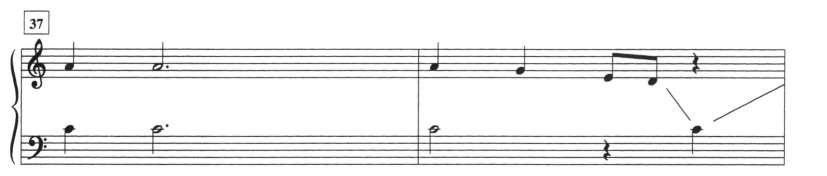

SECONDO

PRIMO

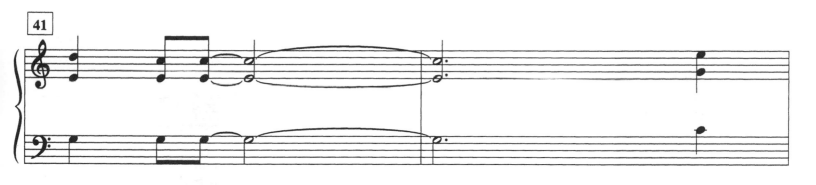

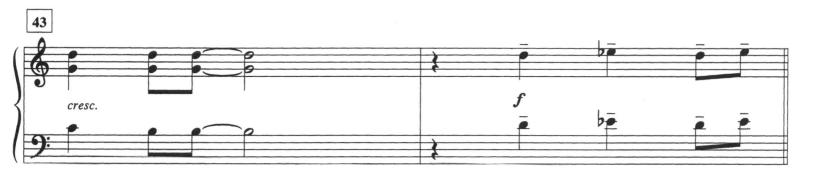

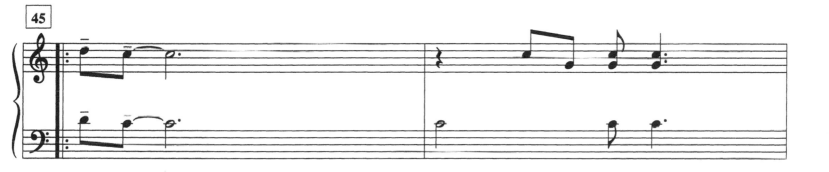

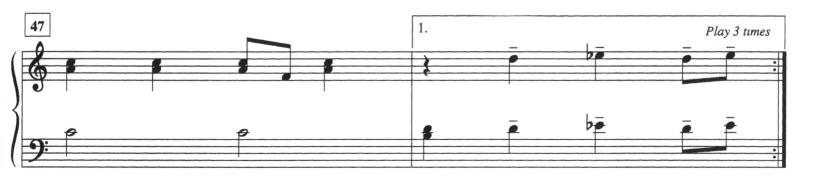

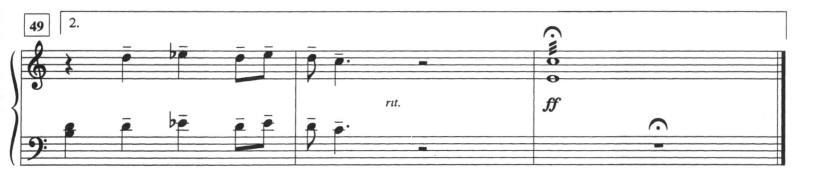

SOMEDAY
from Walt Disney's THE HUNCHBACK OF NOTRE DAME
SECONDO

Music by ALAN MENKEN
Lyrics by STEPHEN SCHWARTZ

SOMEDAY
from Walt Disney's THE HUNCHBACK OF NOTRE DAME
PRIMO

Music by ALAN MENKEN
Lyrics by STEPHEN SCHWARTZ

SECONDO

PRIMO

A SPOONFUL OF SUGAR
from Walt Disney's MARY POPPINS

SECONDO

Words and Music by RICHARD M SHERMAN
and ROBERT B. SHERMAN

A Spoonful of Sugar
from Walt Disney's MARY POPPINS

PRIMO

Words and Music by RICHARD M. SHERMAN
and ROBERT B. SHERMAN

Brightly

Both hands 8va throughout

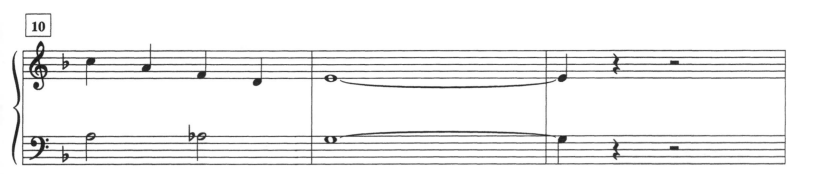

SECONDO

PRIMO

SECONDO

PRIMO

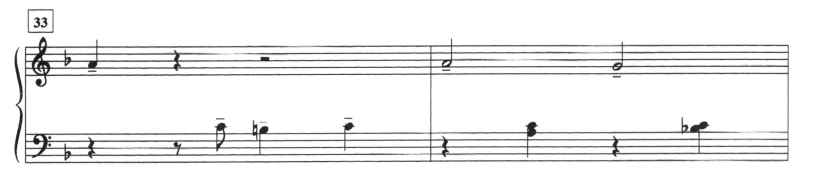

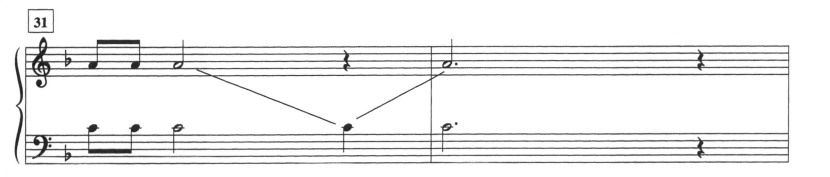

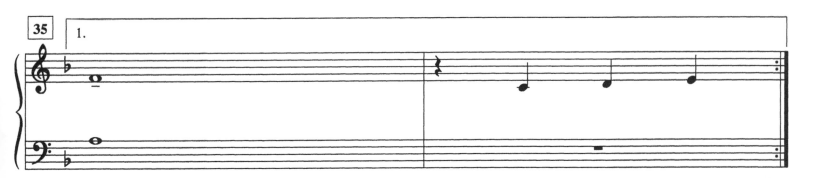

WINNIE THE POOH

from Walt Disney's THE MANY ADVENTURES OF WINNIE THE POOH

SECONDO

Words and Music by RICHARD M. SHERMAN
and ROBERT B. SHERMAN

Tenderly

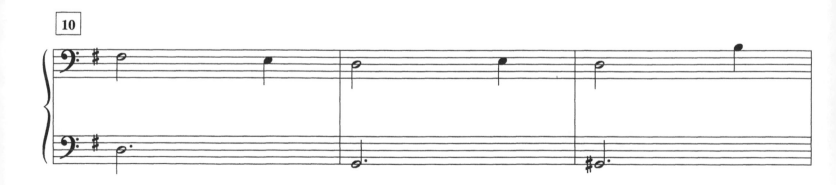

WINNIE THE POOH

from Walt Disney's THE MANY ADVENTURES OF WINNIE THE POOH

PRIMO

Words and Music by RICHARD M. SHERMAN
and ROBERT B. SHERMAN

SECONDO

PRIMO

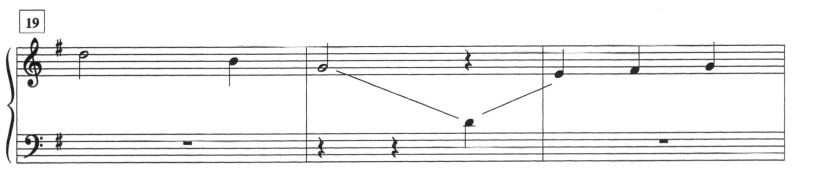

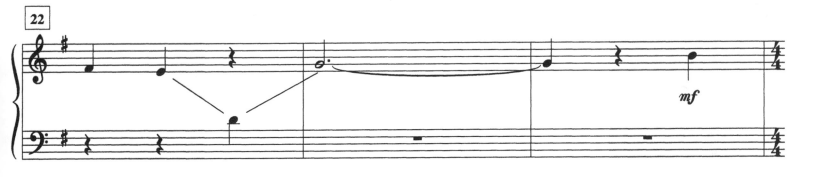

SECONDO

PRIMO

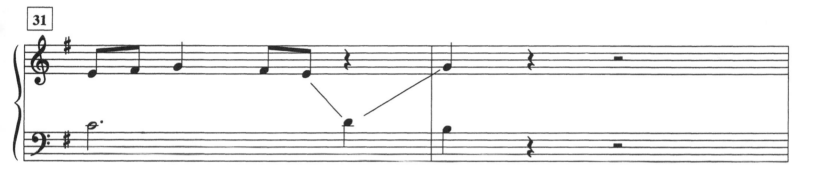

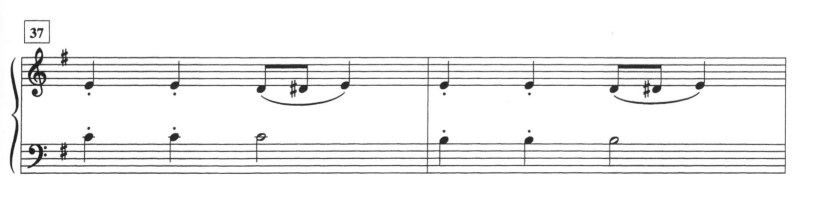

SECONDO

ZIP-A-DEE-DOO-DAH
from Walt Disney's SONG OF THE SOUTH

SECONDO

Words by RAY GILBERT
Music by ALLIE WRUBEL

Brightly

ZIP-A-DEE-DOO-DAH
from Walt Disney's SONG OF THE SOUTH

PRIMO

Words by RAY GILBERT
Music by ALLIE WRUBEL

Brightly
Both hands 8va throughout

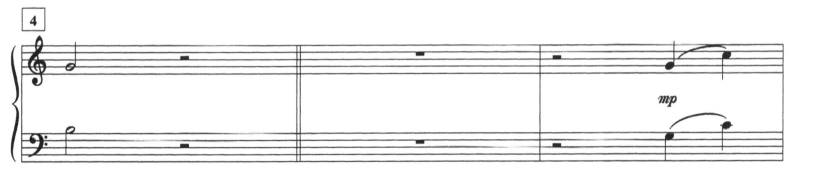

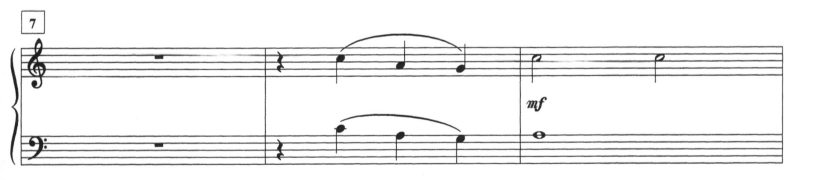

SECONDO

PRIMO

SECONDO

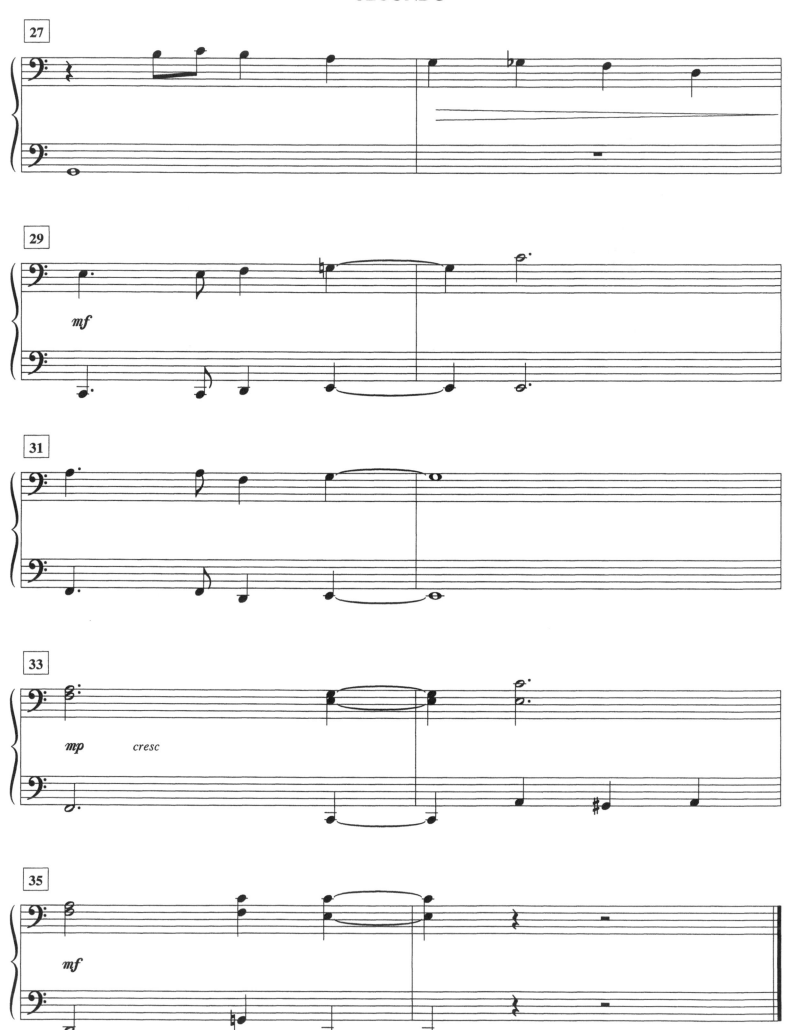